Cake Mix Magic

**Publications International, Ltd.**
Favorite Brand Name Recipes at www.fbnr.com

**Pictured on the front cover** *(clockwise from top left):* Chocolate Peanut Butter Cups *(page 38)*, Chocolate Cherry Torte *(page 90)*, Chocolate Banana Cake *(page 33)* and Strawberry Vanilla Cake *(page 86)*.

**Pictured on the back cover** *(clockwise from top left):* Cheesecake-Topped Brownies *(page 60)*, Individual Cheesecake Cups *(page 76)*, Fudgy Ripple Cake *(page 26)* and Chocolate Chip 'n Oatmeal Cookies *(page 56)*.

**Microwave Cooking:** Microwave ovens vary in wattage. Use the cooking times as guidelines and check for doneness before adding more time.

**Preparation/Cooking Times:** Preparation times are based on the approximate amount of time required to assemble the recipe before cooking, baking, chilling or serving. These times include preparation steps such as measuring, chopping and mixing. The fact that some preparations and cooking can be done simultaneously is taken into account. Preparation of optional ingredients and serving suggestions is not included.

# Cake Mix Magic

# Baking Secrets

## The Basics

It doesn't take a magician to make delicious treats! Simply follow these guidelines for successful baking.

• Read the entire recipe before beginning to make sure you have all the necessary ingredients and baking utensils.

• Remove butter, margarine and cream cheese from the refrigerator to soften, if necessary.

• Toast and chop nuts, pare and slice fruit, and melt chocolate before preparing the batter or dough.

• Measure all the ingredients accurately and assemble them in the order they are called for in the recipe.

• Always use the pan size specified in the recipe, and prepare the pan as directed in the recipe.

• When substituting glass bakeware in recipes that call for baking pans, reduce the oven temperature by 25°F.

• Adjust the oven racks and preheat the oven. Check the oven temperature for accuracy with an oven thermometer.

## The Perfect Pan

**Baking Pan:** Metal baking pans are square, rectangular or round, and have straight sides at least 1½ inches high. The most common sizes are 8- and 9-inch square or round; 11×7×2 inches; and 13×9×2 inches. Baking pans (sometimes referred to as cake pans) are designed for cakes and bar cookies. Shiny aluminum pans are ideal for producing a tender, lightly browned cake crust.

**Baking Sheet:** A baking sheet (often referred to as a cookie sheet) is a flat, rigid sheet of metal on which stiff dough is baked into cookies, rolls, biscuits, etc. It has a low lip on one or more sides for ease in handling; a lip higher than one-half inch interferes with surface browning, especially of cookies. The type of surface also determines the browning characteristics of the baking sheet. Shiny finishes promote even browning. Dark metal baking sheets absorb more heat and can cause food to brown too quickly. Insulated baking sheets have a layer of air sandwiched between two sheets of aluminum which helps to prevent excess browning, but increases baking time. (Some cookie doughs may also spread more on these sheets.) Nonstick finishes minimize sticking and make cleanup easier.

## Measuring Magic

**Dry Ingredients:** Always use standardized measuring spoons and cups. Fill the appropriate measuring spoon or cup to overflowing, and level it off with a metal spatula or the flat edge of a knife.

**Liquid Ingredients:** Use a standardized glass or plastic measuring cup with a pouring spout and calibrations marked on the side. Place the cup on a flat surface, fill to the desired mark, and check the measurement at eye level.

# Charming Classics

## *Philadelphia® Marble Brownies*

- **1 package (21½ ounces) brownie mix**
- **1 package (8 ounces) PHILADELPHIA® Cream Cheese, softened**
- **⅓ cup sugar**
- **½ teaspoon vanilla**
- **1 egg**
- **1 cup BAKER'S® Semi-Sweet Real Chocolate Chips**

**PREPARE** brownie mix as directed on package. Spread in greased 13×9-inch baking pan.

**MIX** cream cheese, sugar and vanilla until well blended. Add egg; mix well. Pour over brownie mixture; swirl with knife. Sprinkle with chips.

**BAKE** at 350°F for 35 to 40 minutes or until cream cheese mixture is lightly browned. Cool in pan on wire rack. Cut into squares.     *Makes 24 brownies*

*Philadelphia® Marble Brownies*

## Orange Pecan Gems

**1 package DUNCAN HINES®
Moist Deluxe® Orange
Supreme Cake Mix**
**1 container (8 ounces) vanilla
low fat yogurt**
**1 egg**
**2 tablespoons butter or
margarine, softened**
**1 cup finely chopped pecans**
**1 cup pecan halves**

*1.* Preheat oven to 350°F. Grease cookie sheets.

*2.* Combine cake mix, yogurt, egg, butter and chopped pecans in large bowl. Beat at low speed with electric mixer until blended. Drop by rounded teaspoonfuls 2 inches apart onto prepared cookie sheets. Press pecan half onto center of each cookie. Bake at 350°F for 11 to 13 minutes or until golden brown. Cool 1 minute on cookie sheets. Remove to cooling racks. Cool completely. Store in airtight container.

*Makes 4½ to 5 dozen cookies*

*Orange Pecan Gems*

## Easy Carrot Cake

1¼ cups **MIRACLE WHIP**® **Salad Dressing**
1 **two-layer yellow cake mix**
4 **eggs**
¼ **cup cold water**
2 **teaspoons ground cinnamon**
2 **cups finely shredded carrots**
½ **cup chopped walnuts**
1 **(16-ounce) container ready-to-spread cream cheese frosting**

• **PREHEAT** oven to 350°F.

• **BEAT** salad dressing, cake mix, eggs, water and cinnamon in large bowl with electric mixer at medium speed until well blended. Stir in carrots and walnuts.

• **POUR** batter into lightly greased 13×9-inch baking pan.

• **BAKE** 35 to 40 minutes or until wooden toothpick inserted in center comes out clean. Cool completely. Spread cake with frosting. Garnish as desired.

*Makes 12 servings*

**Prep Time:** 15 minutes
**Bake Time:** 35 minutes

## Creamy Lemon Bars

1 **package (2-layer size) lemon cake mix**
3 **large eggs, divided**
½ **cup oil**
2 **packages (8 ounces each) PHILADELPHIA**® **Cream Cheese, softened**
1 **container (8 ounces) BREAKSTONE'S**® *or* **KNUDSEN**® **Sour Cream**
½ **cup granulated sugar**
1 **teaspoon grated lemon peel**
1 **tablespoon lemon juice Powdered sugar**

**MIX** cake mix, 1 egg and oil. Press mixture onto bottom and up sides of greased 15×10×1-inch baking pan. Bake at 350°F for 10 minutes.

**BEAT** cream cheese with electric mixer on medium speed until smooth. Add remaining 2 eggs, sour cream, granulated sugar, peel and juice; mix until blended. Pour batter into crust.

**BAKE** at 350°F for 30 to 35 minutes or until filling is just set in center and edges are light golden brown. Cool. Sprinkle with powdered sugar. Cut into bars. Store leftovers in refrigerator.

*Makes 2 dozen bars*

## Streusel Coffeecake

**32 CHIPS AHOY!® Chocolate**
**Chip Cookies, divided**
**1 (18- to 18.5-ounce) package**
**yellow or white cake mix**
**½ cup sour cream**
**½ cup PLANTERS® Pecans,**
**chopped**
**½ cup flaked coconut**
**¼ cup packed brown sugar**
**1 teaspoon ground cinnamon**
**⅓ cup butter, melted**
**Powdered sugar glaze,**
**optional**

*1.* Coarsely chop 20 cookies; finely crush remaining 12 cookies. Set aside.

*2.* Prepare cake mix batter according to package directions; stir in sour cream and chopped cookies. Pour into greased and floured 13×9×2-inch baking pan.

*3.* Mix cookie crumbs, pecans, coconut, brown sugar and cinnamon. Stir in butter; sprinkle over cake batter.

*4.* Bake at 350°F for 40 minutes or until toothpick inserted in center of cake comes out clean. Cool completely. Drizzle with glaze, if desired.          *Makes 24 servings*

## Swiss Chocolate Crispies

**1 package DUNCAN HINES®**
**Moist Deluxe® Swiss**
**Chocolate Cake Mix**
**½ cup shortening plus**
**additional for greasing**
**½ cup butter or margarine,**
**softened**
**2 eggs**
**2 tablespoons water**
**3 cups crispy rice cereal,**
**divided**

*1.* Combine cake mix, ½ cup shortening, butter, eggs and water in large bowl. Beat at low speed with electric mixer for 2 minutes. Fold in 1 cup cereal. Refrigerate 1 hour.

*2.* Crush remaining 2 cups cereal into coarse crumbs.

*3.* Preheat oven to 350°F. Grease cookie sheets. Shape dough into 1-inch balls. Roll in crushed cereal. Place on cookie sheets about 1 inch apart.

*4.* Bake 11 to 13 minutes. Cool 1 minute on cookie sheets. Remove to wire racks.
          *Makes 4 dozen cookies*

*Streusel Coffeecake*

## Brownie Cake Delight

**1 package fudge brownie mix**
**⅓ cup strawberry all-fruit spread**
**2 cups thawed nondairy whipped topping**
**¼ teaspoon almond extract**
**2 cups strawberries, stems removed, halved**
**¼ cup chocolate sauce**

*1.* Prepare brownies according to package directions, substituting 11×7-inch baking pan. Cool completely in pan.

*2.* Whisk fruit spread in small bowl until smooth.

*3.* Combine whipped topping and almond extract in bowl.

*4.* Cut brownie horizontally in half. Place half of brownie on serving dish. Spread with fruit spread and 1 cup whipped topping. Place second half of brownie, cut side down, over bottom layer. Spread with remaining whipped topping. Place strawberries on whipped topping. Drizzle chocolate sauce over cake before serving. Garnish as desired.        *Makes 16 servings*

## Snickerdoodles

**3 tablespoons sugar**
**1 teaspoon ground cinnamon**
**1 package DUNCAN HINES® Moist Deluxe® Yellow Cake Mix**
**2 eggs**
**¼ cup vegetable oil**

*1.* Preheat oven to 375°F. Grease cookie sheets. Place sheets of foil on countertop for cooling cookies.

*2.* Combine sugar and cinnamon in small bowl.

*3.* Combine cake mix, eggs and oil in large bowl. Stir until well blended. Shape dough into 1-inch balls. Roll in cinnamon-sugar mixture. Place balls 2 inches apart on cookie sheets. Flatten balls with bottom of glass.

*4.* Bake at 375°F for 8 to 9 minutes or until set. Cool one minute on cookie sheets. Remove to foil to cool completely.
        *Makes 3 dozen cookies*

*Brownie Cake Delight*

## Golden Gingersnaps

**1 package DUNCAN HINES®
  Golden Sugar Cookie Mix
1 egg
1 tablespoon water
1 tablespoon light molasses
1½ teaspoons ground ginger
1 teaspoon ground cinnamon
½ teaspoon baking soda
¼ cup granulated sugar
1 tablespoon milk
⅓ cup finely chopped pecans**

*1.* Preheat oven to 375°F. Grease cookie sheets.

*2.* Combine cookie mix, egg, water, molasses, ginger, cinnamon and baking soda in large bowl. Stir until thoroughly blended. Drop by level tablespoonfuls into sugar. Roll to completely cover. Place 2 inches apart on prepared cookie sheets. Flatten slightly with bottom of drinking glass. Brush tops lightly with milk. Sprinkle with pecans. Bake 9 minutes for chewy cookies or 10 minutes for crisp cookies. Cool 2 minutes on cookie sheets. Remove to cooling racks. Cool completely. Store in airtight container.

*Makes 3 dozen cookies*

## Pumpkin Snack Bars

*Cake*

**1 package (2-layer size) spice
  cake mix
1 can (16 ounces) pumpkin
¾ cup MIRACLE WHIP® *or*
  MIRACLE WHIP® LIGHT
  Dressing
3 eggs**

*Frosting*

**3½ cups powdered sugar
½ cup (1 stick) butter, softened
2 tablespoons milk
1 teaspoon vanilla**

*Cake*

• **BLEND** cake mix, pumpkin, dressing and eggs with electric mixer on medium speed until well blended. Pour into greased 15×10×1-inch baking pan.

• **BAKE** at 350°F 18 to 20 minutes or until toothpick inserted in center comes out clean. Cool completely on wire rack.

*Frosting*

• **BLEND** all ingredients with electric mixer on low speed until moistened. Beat on high speed until light and fluffy. Spread over cake. *Makes 3 dozen bars*

*Golden Gingersnaps*

## Black Forest Cake

**MAZOLA NO STICK®**
**Cooking Spray**
1 package (18.25 ounces) chocolate cake mix plus ingredients as label directs
Fluffy Frosting (recipe follows)
1 can (21 ounces) cherry pie filling
1 tablespoon cherry flavor liqueur (optional)
2 egg whites

*1.* Preheat oven to 350°F. Spray 2 (9-inch) round cake pans with cooking spray.

*2.* Prepare and bake cake mix according to package directions for 2 (9-inch) round layers. Cool on wire rack 10 minutes. Remove from pans; cool completely.

*3.* Prepare Fluffy Frosting. Place one layer right side up on cake plate. Spoon 1-inch-thick ring of Fluffy Frosting around cake edge.

*4.* Combine cherry pie filling and liqueur; spoon half onto cake layer, inside frosting ring.

*5.* Top with second cake layer, bottom side up. Spread a thin layer of frosting over top of cake.

*6.* Spread a 2-inch-wide ring of frosting around top edge of cake; generously frost side of cake with remaining frosting. Spoon remaining cherry filling on top of cake, inside frosting.

*Makes 12 servings*

## Fluffy Frosting

2 egg whites
⅛ teaspoon salt
1 cup KARO® Light Corn Syrup
¼ cup sugar
1½ teaspoons vanilla

*1.* In large bowl with mixer at high speed, beat egg whites and salt until soft peaks form.

*2.* In small saucepan combine corn syrup and sugar. Stirring constantly, cook over medium-low heat until sugar dissolves and mixture comes to full boil. Remove from heat.

*3.* Beating constantly, pour hot syrup into egg whites in a fine steady stream. Beat in vanilla. Continue beating until mixture holds stiff peaks. Use immediately. Makes enough to frost a two-layer 8- or 9-inch cake.

*Makes about 2 cups*

*Black Forest Cake*

## Crispy Thumbprint Cookies

**1 package (18.25 ounces)
  yellow cake mix**
**½ cup vegetable oil**
**¼ cup water**
**1 egg**
**3 cups crisp rice cereal,
  crushed**
**½ cup chopped walnuts**
**6 tablespoons raspberry
  preserves**

*1.* Preheat oven to 375°F.

*2.* Combine cake mix, oil, water and egg. Beat at medium speed of electric mixer until well blended. Add cereal and walnuts; mix until well blended.

*3.* Drop by heaping teaspoonfuls 2 inches apart onto ungreased baking sheets. Use thumb to make indentation in each cookie. Spoon about ½ teaspoon preserves into center of each cookie.

*4.* Bake 9 to 11 minutes or until golden brown. Cool cookies 1 minute on baking sheet; remove from baking sheet to wire rack to cool completely.

*Makes 3 dozen cookies*

## Gelatin Poke Cake

**1 package (2-layer size) white
  cake mix or cake mix with
  pudding in the mix**
**1 cup boiling water**
**1 package (4-serving size)
  JELL-O® Brand Gelatin
  Dessert, any flavor**
**½ cup cold water**
**1 tub (8 ounces) COOL
  WHIP® Whipped Topping,
  thawed**

**HEAT** oven to 350°F.

**PREPARE** and bake cake mix as directed on package for 13×9-inch baking pan. Remove from oven. Cool cake in pan 15 minutes. Pierce cake with large fork at ½-inch intervals.

**MEANWHILE,** stir boiling water into gelatin in medium bowl at least 2 minutes until completely dissolved. Stir in cold water; carefully pour over cake. Refrigerate 3 hours.

**FROST** with whipped topping. Refrigerate at least 1 hour or until ready to serve. Decorate as desired.     *Makes 15 servings*

*Crispy Thumbprint Cookies*

## *Dump Cake*

**1 (20-ounce) can crushed pineapple with juice, undrained**
**1 (21-ounce) can cherry pie filling**
**1 package DUNCAN HINES® Moist Deluxe® Yellow Cake Mix**
**1 cup chopped pecans or walnuts**
**½ cup (1 stick) butter or margarine, cut into thin slices**

*1.* Preheat oven to 350°F. Grease 13×9-inch pan.

*2.* Dump pineapple with juice into pan. Spread evenly. Dump in pie filling. Spread evenly. Sprinkle cake mix evenly over cherry layer. Sprinkle pecans over cake mix. Dot with butter. Bake 50 minutes or until top is lightly browned. Serve warm or at room temperature.

*Makes 12 to 16 servings*

*Tip:* You can use DUNCAN HINES® Moist Deluxe® Pineapple Supreme Cake Mix in place of Moist Deluxe® Yellow Cake Mix.

## *Quick Peanut Butter Chocolate Chip Cookies*

**1 package DUNCAN HINES® Moist Deluxe® Classic Yellow Cake Mix**
**½ cup creamy peanut butter**
**½ cup butter or margarine, softened**
**2 eggs**
**1 cup milk chocolate chips**

*1.* Preheat oven to 350°F. Grease cookie sheets.

*2.* Combine cake mix, peanut butter, butter and eggs in large bowl. Mix at low speed with electric mixer until blended. Stir in chocolate chips.

*3.* Drop by rounded teaspoonfuls onto prepared cookie sheets. Bake 9 to 11 minutes or until lightly browned. Cool 2 minutes on cookie sheets. Remove to cooling racks.

*Makes 4 dozen cookies*

*Tip:* Crunchy peanut butter may be substituted for regular peanut butter.

*Dump Cake*

# Abracadabra Cakes

## Celebration Pumpkin Cake

- **1 package (18 ounces) spice cake mix**
- **1 can (16 ounces) pumpkin**
- **3 eggs**
- **¼ cup butter, softened**
- **1½ tubs (16 ounces each) cream cheese frosting**
- **⅓ cup caramel ice cream topping**
- **Pecan halves for garnish**

Preheat oven to 350°F. Grease and flour 3 (9-inch) round cake pans. Combine cake mix, pumpkin, eggs and butter in bowl; beat 2 minutes. Divide batter among prepared pans. Bake 20 to 25 minutes or until toothpick inserted in centers comes out clean. Cool 5 minutes on wire rack. Remove from pans; cool completely. Place one cake layer on serving plate; top with frosting. Repeat layers, ending with frosting. Frost cake side. Spread caramel over cake top. Garnish with pecans. *Makes 16 servings*

*Celebration Pumpkin Cake*

### Fudgy Ripple Cake

- **1 package (18.25 ounces) yellow cake mix plus ingredients to prepare mix**
- **1 package (3 ounces) cream cheese, softened**
- **2 tablespoons unsweetened cocoa powder**
- **Fudgy Glaze (recipe follows)**
- **½ cup "M&M's"® Chocolate Mini Baking Bits**

Preheat oven to 350°F. Grease and flour 10-inch bundt pan; set aside. Prepare cake batter as package directs. In bowl mix 1½ cups batter, cream cheese and cocoa powder until smooth. Pour half of yellow batter into prepared pan. Drop spoonfuls of chocolate batter over yellow batter in pan. Top with remaining yellow batter. Bake about 45 minutes or until toothpick inserted in center comes out clean. Cool on wire rack.

Invert cake onto serving plate. Prepare Fudgy Glaze; spread over cake, allowing some to run over side. Sprinkle with "M&M's"® Chocolate Mini Baking Bits.

*Makes 10 servings*

### Fudgy Glaze

- **1 square (1 ounce) semi-sweet chocolate**
- **1 cup powdered sugar**
- **⅓ cup unsweetened cocoa powder**
- **3 tablespoons milk**
- **½ teaspoon vanilla extract**

Place chocolate in small microwave-safe bowl. Microwave at HIGH 30 seconds; stir. Repeat as necessary until chocolate is melted, stirring at 10-second intervals; set aside. In medium bowl combine powdered sugar and cocoa powder. Stir in milk, vanilla and chocolate until smooth.

### Magical Tip

*To soften cream cheese quickly, remove it from the wrapper and place it on a microwave-safe plate. Microwave at MEDIUM (50% power) 15 to 20 seconds or until softened.*

*Fudgy Ripple Cake*

## Fantasy Angel Food Cake

**1 package DUNCAN HINES®
Angel Food Cake Mix
Red and green food coloring
1 container DUNCAN HINES®
Cream Cheese Frosting**

*1.* Preheat oven to 350°F.

*2.* Prepare cake following package directions. Divide batter into thirds and place in 3 different bowls. Add a few drops red food coloring to one. Add a few drops green food coloring to another. Stir each until blended. Leave third one plain. Spoon pink batter into ungreased 10-inch tube pan. Cover with white batter and top with green batter. Bake and cool following package directions.

*3.* To make glaze, heat frosting in microwave at HIGH (100% power) 20 to 30 seconds. Do not overheat. Stir until smooth. Set aside ¼ cup warm glaze. Spoon remaining glaze on top and side of cake to cover. Divide remaining glaze in half and place in 2 bowls. Add a few drops red food coloring to one. Add a few drops green food coloring to the other. Stir each until blended. Drizzle green glaze around cake edge so it runs down side. Repeat with pink glaze.

*Makes 16 servings*

## Cran-Lemon Coffee Cake

**1 package (18.25 ounces)
yellow cake mix with
pudding in the mix
1 cup water
⅓ cup butter, melted
¼ cup fresh lemon juice
3 eggs
1 tablespoon grated lemon
peel
1½ cups chopped cranberries**

• Preheat oven to 350°F. Grease and flour 12-inch tube pan. Beat cake mix, water, butter, lemon juice, eggs and lemon peel in bowl until well blended. Fold in cranberries. Spread batter in pan.

• Bake about 55 minutes or until toothpick inserted in center comes out clean. Cool on wire rack about 10 minutes. Remove from pan; let cool. *Makes 12 servings*

*Fantasy Angel Food Cake*

## Pecan Spice Cake

**MAZOLA NO STICK®**
**Cooking Spray**
**1 package (18.25 ounces)**
**spice cake mix plus**
**ingredients as label directs**
**½ cup finely chopped pecans**
**Coconut-Pecan Filling**
**(recipe follows)**
**Luscious Chocolate Frosting**
**(recipe follows)**

*1.* Preheat oven to 350°F. Spray 2 (9-inch) round cake pans with cooking spray. Prepare cake mix as label directs; stir in pecans. Pour batter into pans.

*2.* Bake as directed. Cool on wire racks 10 minutes. Remove from pans; cool completely. When cool, split layers horizontally in half.

*3.* Place one cake layer on serving plate. Spread with ⅓ of Coconut-Pecan Filling. Top with second cake layer; spread with about ⅔ cup Luscious Chocolate Frosting. Top with third cake layer; spread with ⅓ of filling. Top with fourth cake layer. Frost side of cake with remaining frosting; spread top of cake with remaining filling. Refrigerate 2 hours or until set.

*Makes 12 to 16 servings*

## Coconut-Pecan Filling

**½ cup KARO® Light Corn Syrup**
**¾ cup sugar**
**½ cup evaporated milk**
**½ cup (1 stick) butter**
**3 egg yolks, slightly beaten**
**1 teaspoon vanilla**
**1⅓ cups flaked coconut**
**1 cup finely chopped pecans**

In saucepan mix corn syrup, sugar, milk, butter, egg yolks and vanilla. Cook and stir over medium heat until thickened, 10 to 12 minutes. Remove from heat. Stir in coconut and pecans. Cool until thick and spreadable.      *Makes 2¼ cups*

## Luscious Chocolate Frosting

**1 package (3 ounces) cream**
**cheese**
**¼ cup KARO® Light Corn Syrup**
**2 tablespoons butter**
**2 cups confectioners' sugar**
**⅓ cup unsweetened cocoa**
**½ teaspoon vanilla**

In bowl beat cream cheese, corn syrup and butter until creamy. Beat in confectioners' sugar, cocoa and vanilla until frosting is of spreading consistency.      *Makes 1⅓ cups*

*Pecan Spice Cake*